# Bible Dads and Lads

Brian Ogden

Illustrated by Beccy Blake

Scripture Union

© Brian Ogden 2001

First published 2001

Scripture Union, 207–209 Queensway, Bletchley, Milton Keynes, MK2 2EB, England.

ISBN 1 85999 493 8

British Library Cataloguing-in-Publication Data.
A catalogue record of this book is available from the British Library.

Printed and bound in Great Britain by
Creative Print and Design (Wales) Ebbw Vale.

# Contents

those animals on my own!"

Nothing would change Dad's mind. He was going to do what God had told him. The next day Dad took us into the forest and he chose the trees he wanted.

Wake up Shem! The tree's falling.

After a lot of hard work we cut down all the trees we needed. Then we started to build the ship. We sawed and we nailed and we hammered. Then we had to cover it with tar to make it waterproof. Some of our neighbours came over and looked at what we were doing. They laughed at us.

"Going on a cruise, are you?" they asked.

Dad told us not to take any notice of them.

"Just get the job done," he said.

We built the ship with three decks. On one side there was a big door.

"That's for the animals," said Dad. "We'll never get them in or out otherwise. God thinks of everything."

At long last we put the roof on and the ship was finished.

Then the fun really started. We had to find pairs of all the animals and birds. Some of them, like the sheep and camels and horses, weren't too difficult. It was much harder to catch the lions and cheetahs and elephants. We had to be very careful with some of the snakes. They were really dangerous.

But it wasn't just getting the animals – there was more to do. We had to store enough food for all of them as well.

When all the animals were on the ship, Dad called us together.

"God has spoken to me again," he said. "In seven days' time it is going to start raining. It will rain for forty days without stopping. We must say goodbye to our home and go on board our ship."

Dad was right. It rained and rained and rained. Soon our little ship was floating. After forty days of rain even the mountains were covered with water. The animals got a bit restless. When the rain stopped we brought them on deck for fresh air.

One day, after floating about for weeks, we had a surprise. There was a sudden bump. Our ship had hit the top of a mountain! Everyone was a bit shaken but it did mean the water was going down.

It took a very long time but at long last the ground was dry. It was time to let the animals go. We were really sorry to say goodbye to them. They had become our friends. They were so happy to be on dry land again and soon went off to find new homes. As we went off to rebuild our homes, we thanked God for saving our lives.

We said farewell to the Ark and went off to build new homes. It had been an amazing adventure and we never stopped thanking and praising God for saving our lives. He is truly a great God.

My story doesn't quite end there. God promised that he would never flood the earth again. As a sign of his promise he made a wonderful rainbow. Every time I see a rainbow I remember his promise – I wonder if you do?

After that adventure my brothers and I never doubted Dad again. When God spoke to him, he listened.

**You can find this story in Genesis, chapter 6.**

## Chapter Two

# Dreams and schemes

My name is Jacob and I'm now quite an old man. I live with my sons in the land of Canaan. My sons are shepherds who work hard looking after our flocks of sheep and goats. I love all my sons, all twelve of them. I know I shouldn't have a favourite son but I have to tell you that Joseph is very special to me. You see, Joseph was born in my old age and he is the one I love more than any of the others.

One day, I called him over.

I knew the other boys wouldn't like it. They were jealous of Joseph.

Sadly, the others became really unkind to Joseph – they said some very nasty things whenever they spoke to him. Then Joseph himself made things even worse. He started to tell them about the strange dreams he had been having.

"It was like this," he said, "we were out in the field tying up bundles of wheat. Suddenly my bundle stood up and yours bowed down to mine."

His brothers were mad at him.

"Do you think you are going to be a king and rule over us?" they said. "Shall we have to call you King Joseph?"

They hated him even more because of his dream. But Joseph didn't learn his lesson, and when he had another dream, he told them about that one too.

I saw the sun, the moon, and eleven stars bowing down to me.

Joseph told me his dream as well. I asked him if he thought that we should all bow down to him. I knew my other sons were very angry with him. I didn't know what to do. I trusted God that no harm would come to Joseph. I sent the other boys off to Shechem to look after our sheep. I hoped that over there they would forget all about it.

But the time came when I needed to know if everything was all right with the flocks. I wasn't happy about it but there was no one else so I had to send Joseph.

It was many years later before I heard what had happened to Joseph. It turns out that his brothers saw him coming from a distance.

They must have known that I had sent him but before Joseph reached them they made a plan. It was a very nasty plan. They planned to kill Joseph and throw his body into one of the deep dry wells. There are lots in this part of the country. His brothers, when they came home, were going to tell me that a wild animal had killed Joseph. I'm sorry to say that it was they who were the wild animals.

Reuben, my eldest son, begged them not to kill Joseph. He suggested that they should leave him down the well – perhaps Reuben thought he might come back later and rescue him. The others agreed. They stripped off Joseph's coat and then dropped him kicking and struggling down into the well. As so often happens, God had other ideas. As the brothers were eating, they saw a group of foreigners in the distance. These foreigners were travelling to Egypt. That gave Judah an idea.

They hung a rope down the well, dragged Joseph out and dusted him down. They sold Joseph, my favourite son, for twenty pieces of silver. These foreigners took Joseph to Egypt and sold him in the slave market. Joseph was bought by one of the king's officers as a slave.

That wasn't the end of his adventures, but all through them Joseph continued to trust in God. Meanwhile my other sons planned what they were

going to tell me. They smeared some
goat's blood on his coat then tore off a
piece.

I knew it at once. It was part of the
coat I had given to Joseph. Perhaps you
can begin to imagine how I felt. This
seemed to be proof that my favourite
son was dead. It looked certain that a
wild animal had killed him in the desert.
It was years later before I heard the
whole story. Joseph wasn't dead after all.

His brothers had sold him as a slave. Our God is truly a wonderful God! After many adventures Joseph became the second most powerful man in the whole of Egypt. How proud I was of him when I saw him again. He was wearing a different coat then!

**You can find this story in Genesis, chapter 37.**

## Chapter Three

# We kept our promise

I really didn't know what to do. Year after year it got worse. The problem was children. We didn't have any children and my wife was getting more and more upset about it. She was just longing to have a baby. By the way, my name is Elkanah, and my wife's name is Hannah. We live in Ramah, a town in the hills, in the country of Ephraim.

Once a year Hannah and I make the journey from Ramah to the town of Shiloh to worship the Lord in the temple there. Hannah used to pray the same prayer every year. She prayed that God would give us a son.

Perhaps this year the Lord will hear your prayer.

But year after year nothing happened. We kept going to Shiloh; Hannah kept praying, but still there was no answer to our prayers. Then one year, when Hannah was even more upset than usual, something wonderful happened. Eli, the old priest at Shiloh, was sitting by the door when Hannah went in. Poor Hannah was crying so much that she could hardly see.

In her prayers, Hannah begged God to hear her. She told God about our desperate hope to have a son. Then she

made a promise — one that was going to
be very hard to keep.

I was getting quite worried because
Hannah carried on praying for a long
time. Old Eli, the priest, was watching
her. She was praying silently but her lips
were moving. Eli thought she must have
had too much to drink.

"Sir, I haven't been drinking,"
Hannah told the old priest. "I have been
telling God how I long for a son."

Eli told Hannah to go home in peace. He could see how much a son would mean to us. You know, I think he prayed for us as well. Hannah was much more cheerful on the journey home. At last she seemed more hopeful.

Some months later there was a great event. The son Hannah and I had prayed for was born. None of our friends had ever seen us so happy. He was a lovely little boy and we called him Samuel. The boy was only a few weeks old when it was time for us to go to Shiloh again. He was too young to travel all that distance. I wasn't happy leaving them at home but I had to go. I

wanted to give thanks to God for his goodness to us both.

Hannah stayed at home that year but she meant us to keep the promise she had made to God. It would be very hard to hand Samuel back to God, but a promise is a promise. A few years later, when Samuel was a little older, Hannah and I took him with us to Shiloh. This time we took some gifts with us as well. Hannah held Samuel's hand and brought him to Eli.

Although there were tears in her eyes, Hannah prayed a lovely prayer.

"The Lord has filled my heart with joy;
How happy I am because of what he
has done.

How joyful I am because God has
helped me!"

It was hard leaving Samuel at Shiloh
with Eli. We talked a lot about it on the
journey home. But Hannah had kept
her promise and she was happy with
what she had done. She never forgot
Samuel. Each year, before our visit to
Shiloh, Hannah worked hard making a
coat for our son. She had to guess how
much he had grown but somehow she
never made a mistake.

I looked forward, as much as Hannah did, to seeing him every year. He was obviously a great help to Eli in the house of the Lord. Eli blessed us every year when we went to worship and see Samuel.

"May the Lord give you other children to take the place of the one you gave to him," he said.

After that Hannah and I did have more children – three more sons and two daughters. But Samuel always remained very special to Hannah and me. We were very proud of him as he grew up. The son we never expected to have became a great man of God.

**You can read this story in 1 Samuel, chapter 1.**

## Chapter Four

# My father and my friend

There are two really important people in my life – one is my father, the other is my best friend. My father's name is Saul – King Saul of the Israelites. My best friend is called David. My name, by the way, is Jonathan. Sadly, though, there's a big problem between my father and David. You see my father doesn't like David. At times he's even tried to kill David. But let me start at the beginning – the time when Saul the king first met David the shepherd boy.

It all started when Dad was leading the army against our enemies, the Philistines. They had a soldier called Goliath. Goliath was huge and all our

soldiers were frightened of him. David, the shepherd boy, was visiting his brothers who were in the army. He knew that God would help him to fight Goliath. To everyone's amazement, he killed Goliath. After that, David became a hero and Dad became very jealous. The ordinary people were saying that David was a better soldier than Dad and Dad didn't like it.

It was after he killed Goliath that David and I became friends.

Dad made David an officer in the army. David was a very brave man and won lots of battles. When he wasn't leading his soldiers against the Philistines David came to our house. He played the harp beautifully. Dad loved harp music – it seemed to take away his bad moods. But one evening Dad acted very strangely. He picked up his spear and threw it at David. David managed to dodge the spear. He got away from the house but from then on things didn't look too good for him.

So there was I in the middle. I loved my dad but I also loved David. David won more battles against the Philistines than any of the other officers. This just seemed to make it worse as far as Dad was concerned. Things got really serious when Dad took me on one side and told me he was going to kill David. That put me on the spot. What do you think I did?

Then I made a secret plan with David.

"David," I said, "tomorrow morning hide in the field by the house. I'll bring Dad out and talk to him about you."

The next morning I reminded Dad about all the good things David had done.

"Dad, it was David who risked his life to kill Goliath," I told him. "He's always done what's best for you. He's a brilliant soldier."

Dad thought about it. I could see it wasn't easy for him.

"I swear by the living Lord that I won't have David killed," he said at last.

I hoped that would be the end of it. I hoped that Dad would see that David just wanted to serve him. I took David back into the house and for a time things settled down. David carried on leading the army against the Philistines. But it wasn't to last.

One night, back from another battle, David came to our house.

As David was playing, the anger returned to Dad. He looked at David then hurled the spear he was holding. He tried to pin David to the wall. David dodged out of the way leaving the spear stuck in the wall. He escaped from the house and ran home.

This time David knew that he couldn't ever come back again. It was just too dangerous. Every time that Dad saw him he tried to kill him. I only managed to see David once more. We were in tears — it's always sad to say goodbye to your best friend.

33

God was with David. Some years later, after my father was killed in battle, my best friend, David, became king.

**You can find the stories about Saul and Jonathan in 1 Samuel, chapters 18–20.**

## Chapter Five

# Never argue with an angel

If there is one thing I have learned in my long life, it is never to argue with an angel! It is not a sensible thing to do. But let me start at the beginning. My name is Zechariah and I am a priest in the great Temple in Jerusalem. My wife's name is Elizabeth. Although we loved and served God, and kept all his laws, we had one great sadness.

How I wish we had a child.

But God is good and all that was about to change. It happened when I was leading the worship during the daily service in the Temple. I was in that part of the Temple where only priests are allowed to go. I lit the incense on the altar. The incense gave off a beautiful smell and there were clouds of smoke. Suddenly through the smoke I saw a figure. At first I thought it must be another priest. But it wasn't a priest!

Well, I was afraid – and so would you have been! The angel had come with a special message for me from God. The message was this: God had answered our prayers and Elizabeth was going to give birth to a son! The angel even told me what we should call our son. His name was to be John. John was to have a very special job – he was to get people ready to hear and follow Jesus.

I found it very hard to believe what the angel had said. I told him that both Elizabeth and I were too old to have a baby. That was a bad mistake and the angel didn't like it. He told me that God had sent him to give me this good news.

"Because you have not believed God, you will be unable to speak. You will remain silent until the day my promise to you comes true," he said.

And silent I was! I couldn't speak a word. The people outside were beginning to wonder why I had been so long. When I came out, and couldn't speak, they knew something had happened.

I made signs to them using my hands – there was nothing else I could do!

When my time in the Temple ended, I went home and tried to explain to Elizabeth what had happened. The angel was right – soon Elizabeth knew she was going to have a baby. Although I couldn't speak, you can imagine how excited we were!

About six months later we had a
visitor. It was Elizabeth's cousin, Mary,
from Nazareth. Just as an angel had told
me about our son, so an angel told Mary
that she too was going to have a baby.
Mary had had the sense not to argue
with him!

It was lovely for Elizabeth to have
someone to talk to. (It wasn't much fun
talking to me – I couldn't answer her!)
Elizabeth and Mary spent many happy
hours chatting about becoming mothers.

After three months Mary went back home to Nazareth and only days later our son was born. He was a fine healthy boy. I was a very proud and happy father.

Our friends and neighbours soon heard the wonderful news and rushed round to our home. It is our custom to give a baby his name when he is a week old.

Our friends and neighbours couldn't understand that – there was no one else in the family called John. So they came and asked me. I made signs for something to write on.

They were surprised about the name but even more surprised when they heard me speak. God had kept his word; I could speak now his promise had come true. Our son, the son we thought we would never have, grew into a great servant of God. He became known as

John the Baptist. I'm sure you've heard of him. As for me – I never argued with an angel again!

**You can read this story in Luke, chapter 1.**

## Chapter Six

# Gone missing

It was then that we knew that Jesus, our son, was missing. I thought Jesus had been walking with Mary, his mother, and she thought he had been with me,

Joseph. As it turned out he was with neither of us.

But let me start my story at the beginning. As you know, we all lived happily in the little town of Nazareth. Every year, it was our custom to travel to Jerusalem for the Passover Festival. This is the most important religious festival of the year. The journey from Nazareth to Jerusalem takes several days. We always travel with friends and relations at Passover – it makes the journey more fun and is safer than travelling on your own.

When Jesus was twelve, he was old enough to go with us for the first time. He had been looking forward to going to the Festival for weeks. We kept talking about it as we worked together in my carpenter's shop.

Jesus was not disappointed when we got there. Jerusalem, our holy city, was crowded with visitors from many countries. I told Jesus where some of them had come from. They were all speaking their own languages and dressed in their own national costumes. There was so much to see and do. I was quite surprised, but Jesus seemed to be most interested when we visited the Temple. He sat and listened to the Jewish teachers. I couldn't understand everything they were saying but he seemed to know what they meant.

All too soon the festival was over and it was time to start our journey home. The women and children, who travelled more slowly, usually went on ahead of the men. The men left later and caught up with the others by the evening meal. I remember that moment well. I found Mary with our friends from Nazareth but there was no sign of Jesus.

Between us, Mary and I asked everyone. But nobody had seen him. There was only one thing for it — Jesus must still be in Jerusalem. As soon as it was daylight, Mary and I hurried back to the city. We searched in the streets, we looked in the shops, we pushed our way through the crowds but still we couldn't find him. Then Mary had an idea.

There, three days after our search began, we found Jesus. He was calmly sitting and listening to the teachers as

they taught the crowd in the Temple.
You can imagine how relieved we were
to see him. But you know what parents
are like – having found him we were a
bit cross.

Jesus smiled at us and then said
something that made us stop and think.
I remembered those words for a long
time afterwards.

"Didn't you know that I had to be in
my Father's house?" he said.

It was as if he now knew that God was his true father, not me. It was a reminder to us that God had some very special plans for him when he grew up. We travelled back to Nazareth and Jesus remained the loving obedient son he had always been. The next few years went by quickly. I was able to share with Jesus some of the skills I had as a carpenter. He learned quickly and was a great help to me.

He didn't only learn from me – he learnt a great deal from our teachers, the rabbi and the Scriptures. Mary and I were very proud of our son.

If Jesus was ever late home, Mary and I told him again the story of his first visit to Jerusalem. We all laughed at it then. All too soon he left my carpentry shop and our home in Nazareth and started the work that God, his Father, sent him to do.

**You will find this story in Luke, chapter 2**

## Chapter Seven

# Fish and ships

My name is Zebedee and I have two fine sons. Their names are James and John. My family has lived for years by the side of Lake Galilee. We have always been fishermen. I remember teaching my boys to fish in the lake as soon as they could handle an oar.

Some people call our lake the Sea of Galilee. It's quite big – about twenty-three kilometres long and eight kilometres wide. The lake has always been good for fishing. Some men fish with hand-held nets in the shallow water by the shore. They spot a shoal of fish and throw the net over them. Some use boats out on the lake. They fish with nets that they drag behind the boat. It was hard work but James and John had learned both ways to fish almost as soon as they could walk. There were other things to understand too.

Lots of families like ours make their living from fishing in the lake. Most of the fish are dried in the sun, packed in salt, and sent to the big towns. James and John have two very good friends – Andrew and Peter. They come from another fishing family and work with James and John.

One day the four friends had a great surprise. The day had started like any other. The boys were washing down their boats after a night on the lake during which they had caught no fish.

There was always plenty to do after a fishing trip – catch or no catch. Nets get snagged on the bottom of the lake and need mending. Boats need cleaning and checking to make sure that they are not leaking. Sails need repairing. Soon the boys saw a crowd beginning to gather by the shore.

The crowd got bigger and started to push down towards the lakeside. The boys were right – it was Jesus. They had all heard Jesus speak before. Then Jesus walked over to Peter. Peter's boat was half in and half out of the water.

Jesus got into the boat and asked
Peter to push off a little from the shore.
It gave Jesus a good high place from
which to speak to the crowd. They
could all see him and hear him. James
and John sat on the side of their boat
and listened hard.

Jesus was the sort of speaker that
everyone wanted to hear. He told such
wonderful stories that even the children
enjoyed them. The crowds followed
him everywhere. The fishermen
stopped mending their nets and cleaning
their boats. The whole crowd went
quiet listening to Jesus. People begged
Jesus to tell them more stories. There
was a sigh when he finished. The crowd
drifted slowly back to their work or to
their homes. Jesus climbed out of the
boat.

Peter started to argue with Jesus. He told Jesus that they had been out on the lake all night but hadn't caught a single fish. Then Jesus looked at Peter. That was enough. James and John launched their boat and joined Peter and Andrew on the lake. Those of us who watched could hardly believe it – they caught so many fish that the two boats almost sank under the weight! I thought we might have to rescue them. I've seen some good catches in my time but never one like that before.

It was one of the last fishing trips the four boys made. I didn't see much of James and John after that. From that moment they were no longer lake fishermen – they were fishing for men. James and John, Peter and Andrew left the lake and became followers of Jesus.

As their father, it was hard for me when James and John left home. But I was very proud of them both. They gave up good jobs to become disciples of Jesus. This meant that they went everywhere with Jesus. They lived with Jesus and they learned from Jesus.

**You can find this story in Luke, chapter 5.**

## Chapter Eight

# Parents, pigs and parties

I suppose it started because I was bored. I had worked on my dad's farm all my life and it was the same thing every day.

I had to milk the cows, feed the sheep, plough the fields and sow the seed. It was hard work and I was getting fed up with it. There had to be something better. Then a friend came to visit us. He told us what fun it was in the city. There was so much to do. No chance of being bored there! That made me think. I knew that half the farm would belong to me when my dad died. The other half would go to my older brother who worked on the farm with Dad and me. One evening, after I had spent the day ploughing, I went to see Dad.

I could see Dad wasn't at all happy about it but he didn't argue. Part of the farm was sold off and he gave me the money. It didn't take me long to pack a few things. Then I said goodbye to Dad, Mum and my brother and left. They all looked rather sad – especially Dad. He gave me a hug before I went and told me to take care of myself.

Think of it – no more getting up early, no more sheep to chase, no more muddy ploughing, no more cows to milk! I was off to the city as fast as I could go.

The first few days were fantastic. I bought some really cool clothes. I went to all-night parties. I didn't bother to get up until midday – I could never do that on the farm! Soon I found I had some new friends. They came with me wherever I went.

After a while my money was beginning to run out. As my money ran out, my new friends ran out as well. Then one day I woke up and looked in my purse. It was empty – I had no money left. I had spent it all! There was nothing for it – I had to get a job or starve. The only work I knew about was farming. I tried lots of farms and was getting desperate. But at last I found a job.

This was the last job I wanted. It's not a nice job looking after pigs. But I had no choice – it was pigs or perish. As I fed the pigs, I began thinking about home. The hungrier I got, the more I thought about my dad's farm. The day I nearly ate some pig food, I made up my mind. The people who work on Dad's farm always have plenty to eat. They never go to bed hungry. I'm going back before I starve to death here! Perhaps Dad will forgive me and give me a job.

It was a long, hard journey home. What made it so hard was knowing how stupid I'd been to leave home in the first place.

I wondered what Dad would say. Would he have me back? Would he let me be one of his servants?

At last, dirty and tired from the journey, I could just see my home on the horizon. Standing outside the house was someone I knew. It was Dad! My dad was actually looking for me! The minute he saw me, he started to run towards me. I didn't know what to do. Was he going to chase me away? I certainly deserved it. I just stood there

Dad, I've done wrong. I'm not fit to be your son.

waiting for him.

I couldn't believe what happened next. He gave me a wonderful hug – just like the one he gave me before I left. Then he gave some orders.

"Hurry!" said Dad. "Look, my son has come home. Get the best clothes you can find for him. Get food ready – we're going to have a party."

I could hardly believe that he had forgiven me for leaving him like that. I told Dad that I didn't deserve any of this. But he wouldn't listen to me. He was just so pleased to see me – to have me home again. My dad is a very forgiving father. I have learnt that having a loving father is much more important than having money. I'll tell you another thing – the party I had at home with the family was much better than any I had in the town!

**You can read this story in Luke, chapter 15.**